Ice Cream Treats

Ice Cream Treats

The Inside Scoop

Paul Fleisher

photographs by David O. Saunders

Carolrhoda Books, Inc./Minneapolis

For Debra and Diane, our favorite sweet treats—P. F. and D. O. S.

The publisher gratefully thanks Good Humor-Breyers Ice Cream for their generous cooperation in the creation of this book. Thanks also to Ann Piehl and Andrew Herbers for the recipe on page 10.

Carolrhoda Books, Inc.
A division of Lerner Publishing Group
241 First Avenue North
Minneapolis, MN 55401 U.S.A.

Website address: www.lernerbooks.com

LIBRARY OF CONGRESS CATALOGING-IN-PUBLICATION DATA

Fleisher, Paul.
    Ice cream treats: the inside scoop / Paul Fleisher ; photographs by David O. Saunders.
        p. cm.
    Includes index.
    ISBN 1-57505-268-7 (lib. bdg. : alk. paper)
    1. Ice cream, ices, etc.—Juvenile literature. [I. Ice cream, ices, etc.]
I. Saunders, David, 1952–   , ill. II. Title.
TX795.F57 2001
641.8'62—dc21   00-009229

Manufactured in the United States of America
1 2 3 4 5 6 – JR – 06 05 04 03 02 01

Contents

The simple pleasure of an ice cream treat—or just a bowl of vanilla with sprinkles on top—can make a kid's day.

Simply Delicious

Do you like ice cream treats? Almost everyone loves to eat sweet, creamy ice cream covered with a crunchy candy coating. It's hard to imagine anything more delicious than smooth vanilla ice cream on a stick, topped with a tasty layer of dark chocolate. Have you ever wondered how these wonderful desserts are made?

Ice cream is a simple food. It's made from milk, cream, sugar, and flavorings such as vanilla, chocolate, or fruit. Some recipes also use eggs. These ingredients are mixed together. Then they're frozen. But making ice cream isn't quite as simple as that. The ingredients have to be frozen in a special way.

Suppose you mixed milk, cream, sugar, and vanilla, and then just put the mixture in the freezer. You wouldn't get ice cream. Instead, you'd get a sweet, milky ice cube. One very important step would be missing. Ice cream won't be smooth and creamy unless you use a special freezer that breaks the ice into millions of tiny crystals as it freezes.

You may have seen someone making homemade ice cream. The liquid ice cream mix is poured into a chilled canister inside the ice cream freezer. In the center of the canister is a paddle called a **dasher.** A hand crank or electric motor turns the dasher, making it spin slowly. As it spins, it stirs the mix. It also scrapes away the ice crystals that form on the inside walls of the freezer. The constant scraping keeps the ice crystals from getting too big. The mix freezes into ice cream instead of a block of ice.

Pouring mix into an ice cream freezer (top) isn't enough to make good ice cream. You'll also need a dasher (left) and a motor or a hand crank to make it spin.

Ice cream also has a secret ingredient that makes it smooth and creamy—air! As the dasher spins, it stirs tiny air bubbles into the mix. When the mix freezes, the bubbles are trapped in the ice cream. They make the ice cream light, soft, and scoopable.

This added air is called **overrun.** In some ice cream, overrun almost doubles the amount of space the ice cream takes up as it freezes. A gallon of liquid ice cream mix makes about 2 gallons of ice cream. So ice cream is almost one-half air. But it's the best air you've ever tasted!

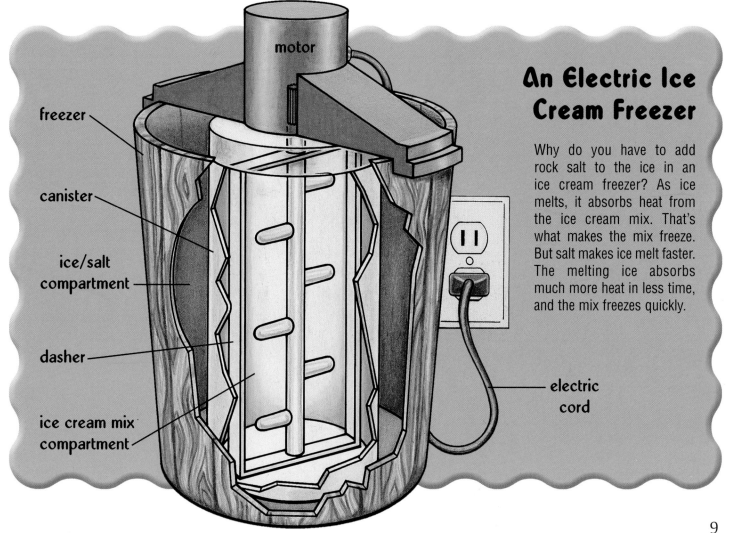

motor

freezer

canister

ice/salt compartment

dasher

ice cream mix compartment

An Electric Ice Cream Freezer

Why do you have to add rock salt to the ice in an ice cream freezer? As ice melts, it absorbs heat from the ice cream mix. That's what makes the mix freeze. But salt makes ice melt faster. The melting ice absorbs much more heat in less time, and the mix freezes quickly.

electric cord

Ice cream factories sometimes add **emulsifiers** and **stabilizers** to their ice cream recipes. Emulsifiers act on the ice cream's **butterfat.** Butterfat is the fat found in milk and cream. Emulsifiers help the butterfat coat the tiny air bubbles that are mixed into the ice cream. This makes the ice cream feel creamier in your mouth. Stabilizers keep large ice crystals from forming while the ice cream is stored. That's important because ice cream may spend several weeks or longer in a supermarket freezer before you take it home.

Of course, people haven't always used emulsifiers and stabilizers. They haven't always had ice cream freezers, either. How did people make this simple dessert hundreds of years ago?

Shake-and-Freeze Ice Cream

Even if you don't have an ice cream maker at home, you can still make a simple kind of ice cream. You will need:

1 cup milk	3–4 cups of ice
3 tablespoons sugar	a pint plastic bag that zips shut
1 teaspoon vanilla	a gallon plastic bag that zips shut
6 tablespoons salt	a pair of gloves

Mix the milk, sugar, and vanilla in a bowl. Pour the mixture carefully into the small bag and seal tightly. Place the salt and ice in the large bag. Place the small bag in the large one. Seal the large bag. Put on the gloves and shake the large bag for about five minutes. Take the small bag out of the larger one. Scoop or pour the ice cream out of the small bag and eat immediately. (For more treats you can make at home, see the recipes on pages 44–45 and 47.)

The Story of Ice Cream

No one knows who invented ice cream. We know that people in ancient China and Rome ate flavored, sweetened ices. Europeans have been eating ice cream since around the 1500s. But for many years, ice cream was a treat for only the wealthiest people. The ice needed to make it had to be stored from the previous winter or brought from high in the mountains. Either way, making ice cream was a very expensive project.

Fetching ice was hard work in the days before freezers.

Luckily, refrigeration was invented in the 1830s. For the first time, a machine could make things cold and keep them that way. Home refrigerators didn't become common until the 1920s, but factories were making and storing ice by the 1850s. This made ice much cheaper and easier to find. So making ice cream became less expensive too. Soon almost anyone could afford to buy a dish of ice cream at an ice cream parlor.

The year 1846 brought a great breakthrough for dessert lovers. An American woman, Nancy Johnson, invented a hand-cranked ice cream freezer. It looked much like the ones we still use. People could finally make ice cream at home. As you might imagine, the new invention was very popular.

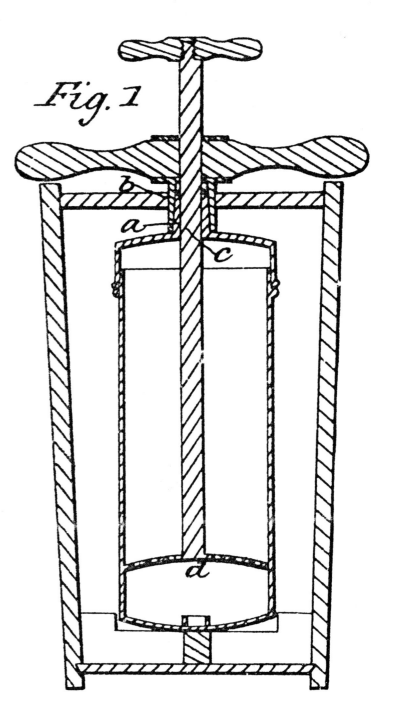

Nancy Johnson's invention helped make ice cream a do-it-yourself treat.

In the early days of ice cream novelties, a nickel could buy you a delicious dessert.

About five years later, a Baltimore dairy owner named Jacob Fussell had a problem. Fussell's dairies were producing more cream than he could sell. He decided to try making ice cream with the leftovers. Before long, he was making more money from ice cream than from milk. He turned his business into a full-time ice cream factory, the first in the United States. Within a few years, factories started opening in other cities. Ice cream was on its way to becoming America's most popular dessert.

What about ice cream treats? In the dairy business, individual ice cream portions are called **novelties.** In 1919, candy store owner Christian Nelson invented a dessert called the I-Scream Bar. The I-Scream Bar was a square block of vanilla ice cream with a thin chocolate coating. It was the first chocolate-covered ice cream novelty. Two years later, Nelson and Russell Stover began selling the messy treats as Eskimo Pies. Right away, they were a huge success.

Meanwhile, an ice cream store owner and candy maker named Harry Burt tried to improve Nelson's idea. Burt put a wooden stick in his ice cream bar, making it easier to hold. He called his invention the Good Humor Ice Cream Sucker. By the mid-1920s, novelties like Good Humor bars and Eskimo Pies were favorites across the United States.

Ice cream has grown even more popular since then. Americans eat about 4 gallons of ice cream a year per person. People eat more ice cream in the United States than in any other country—and a lot of it is in the form of novelties. Where do all those treats come from? Let's visit a factory to see how ice cream treats are made.

The Good Humor Ice Cream Sucker was invented after Harry Burt's other popular treat, a lollipop called the Jolly Boy Sucker. In 1920, he made a square block of ice cream covered with thicker and richer chocolate coating than the I-Scream Bar. His daughter liked the treat but thought it was too messy. She suggested that he put the ice cream on a stick, like his lollipop. Burt agreed, and a classic treat was born.

Harry Burt (above) advertised his Good Humor Ice Cream Sucker as a way to enjoy ice cream without sticky fingers (right).

An Ice Cream Factory

It takes a lot of space to make ice cream. This three-story ice cream factory fills up a whole city block. It has several connected buildings. The factory operates twenty-four hours a day, in three eight-hour shifts. About 250 people work here.

The factory has six **production lines.** A production line is a series of machines that make a product in a factory. Three of the factory's production lines make half-gallons of ice cream. The other three lines make many different kinds of ice cream novelties.

A worker turns a valve to drain milk from a tank truck.

Everything starts in the **loading bays.** Each day, about ten 5,000-gallon tank trucks deliver milk, cream, **condensed milk,** and liquid sugar. Condensed milk is milk that has been thickened by heating. More than half of its water has been removed. Liquid sugar is simply a sugar syrup.

In a different part of the factory, trucks deliver buckets of flavorings. They unload vanilla and chocolate, frozen fruit, and boxes of cookie and candy chips. All the food ingredients are held in freezers or refrigerated rooms to keep them fresh. Still other trucks deliver cleaning supplies.

New deliveries arrive every day. The factory gets only a day or two of supplies at a time. This means the factory doesn't need much extra storage space. It also saves money, because the company doesn't have to pay for large amounts of materials before they're needed.

Henry Butler's job is to receive deliveries from the drivers. He also makes sure the ingredients are handled and stored properly. Some of the milk is fresh from dairy farms. This **raw milk** hasn't been processed at all. It may contain harmful **bacteria.** Bacteria are very tiny living things. Some are helpful to people. But some bacteria can cause milk to spoil or even make people sick.

Dozens of boxes of ingredients must be unloaded, moved, and carefully stored every day.

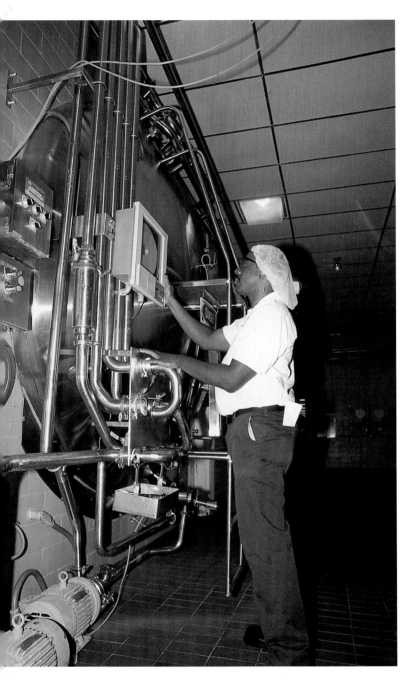

To get rid of any unhealthy bacteria in the raw milk, Eric Worthington **pasteurizes** it. Pasteurization is a process that kills dangerous bacteria in foods. It was named for the French scientist Louis Pasteur. In the 1860s, Pasteur discovered that heating raw milk until it is almost hot enough to boil kills the harmful bacteria. Then the milk is safe for people to drink.

Like all the machines in the factory, the pasteurizer is controlled and monitored by computers. The milk is pumped into long tubes, where it's heated to the right temperature. It's heated just long enough to kill the bacteria.

Checking the settings
of the pasteurizer

Taking a milk sample to send to the quality assurance lab

Too much heat spoils the taste of milk. So as soon as it's pasteurized, the milk is quickly cooled. It's pumped through refrigerated pipes into a huge, refrigerated storage tank.

Eric Worthington sends a sample from each truckload of milk to the factory's **quality assurance lab** for testing. The quality assurance lab is one of the most important places in the factory. Here technicians make sure that each batch of milk is safe to use and will make delicious ice cream.

Quality assurance tests confirm that the milk is safe and perfect for making ice cream.

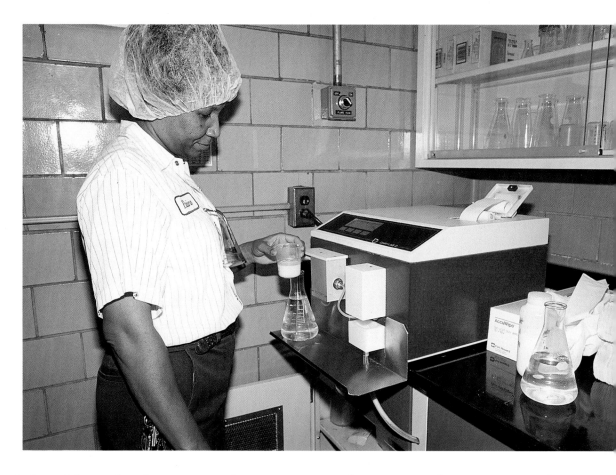

First, technician Elaine King checks to see if the pasteurization has killed all the harmful bacteria. Next she measures the amount of milk solids and butterfat in the milk. Milk solids are the sugars and proteins dissolved in the milk. Butterfat holds much of the flavor in ice cream and makes it feel smooth on your tongue. Except for special fat-free treats, each ice cream recipe must have a certain amount of butterfat. That way, the workers can be sure that each batch will taste equally as good.

The quality assurance lab will check the milk again later to make sure it's safe before it leaves the factory. But by that time, it won't be milk anymore—it will be ice cream.

Safe Work, Safe Treats

You might be surprised to discover that an ice cream factory is very loud. The pumps and other machines make a lot of noise. The workers wear earplugs to protect their hearing. They also wear safety glasses to protect their eyes and steel-toed shoes to protect their feet from anything heavy that might be dropped by accident.

Cleanliness is very important in the factory, too. People who work with the ice cream must wash their hands and dip them in a liquid that kills germs. The workers wear uniforms and hairnets. They can't eat while they're working with the machines or the ice cream, and they can't wear any jewelry. The company doesn't want a customer to find anything but ice cream in an ice cream bar.

Thanks to safety glasses, earplugs, gloves, and a hairnet, this worker is well prepared for a safe day on the job.

A Batch of Ice Cream

The ice cream factory uses a common method called **batch processing.** Ingredients are mixed together in large batches. Each batch then passes through a series of machines. The machines turn the ingredients into a final product. Meanwhile, the workers prepare the next batch of ingredients. Batch processing is the same method other factories use to make all kinds of products, from cookies to concrete blocks.

When it's time to begin making ice cream, P. L. Evans tells the computer what kind to make. The computer measures the milk, cream, and sugar into a 3,000-gallon vat called a **mixing station**. A machine stirs all the ingredients together. Then the mixture is pasteurized again and pumped to a large storage tank.

A computer controls the amount and type of ingredients in each batch of ice cream.

The **production floor** is where all the ingredients are finally turned into tasty treats. The ice cream mix is pumped into gleaming stainless steel **flavor vats.** Each flavor vat holds 250 to 500 gallons of mix. Workers add vanilla and other flavorings to the mix. A spinning steel paddle called an **agitator** stirs the flavorings evenly into the liquid.

From the flavor vats, the ice cream is pumped to a production line. Each of the factory's three novelty production lines processes more than 75 gallons of mix an hour. While the first batch of mix is being made into ice cream, workers will get another batch ready. That way, the production line won't have to stop when one flavor vat is empty. This is how batch processing works.

Inside each of the steel flavor vats on the production floor (above), mix is stirred by an agitator (above left).

The flavored mix is pumped to freezers. The factory's freezers work very much like a home ice cream maker, but they work *much* faster. A network of tubes surrounds each freezer. The tubes carry a liquid called ammonia, which makes the freezer cold.

Liquid mix flows through a steel pipe into one end of the freezer. It enters a cylinder at the freezer's center. Inside this cylinder is a steel dasher. As the dasher spins around, its sharp knives scrape the inner walls of the cylinder and stir tiny ice crystals back into the mix. The dasher also mixes in just the right amount of air.

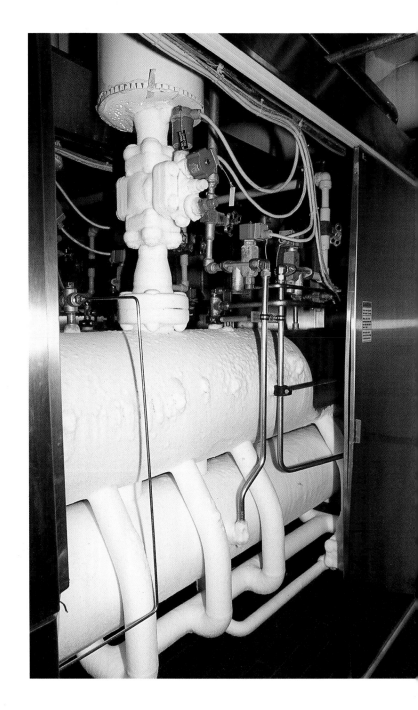

One of the freezers that turns the mix into soft ice cream

Computers control the temperature of the freezing ice cream and the speed of the whirling dasher. By the time it leaves the freezer, the ice cream is frozen. But it's still soft enough to flow through the frost-covered, stainless steel pipes.

Checking the freezer's temperature

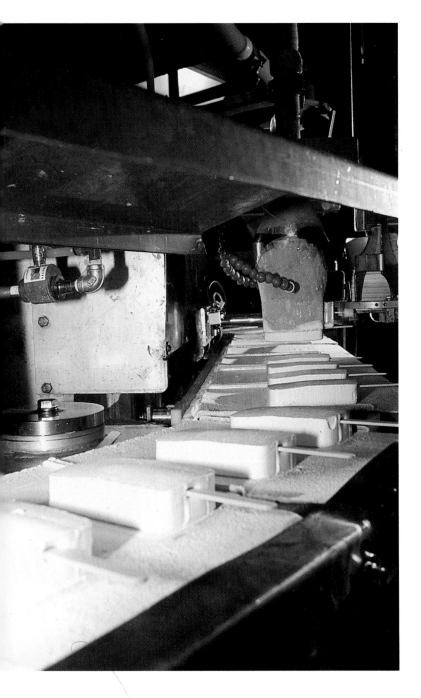

From Ice Cream to Treat

The soft ice cream's next stop is a machine fitted with an **extrusion head.** The extrusion head has an opening shaped like an ice cream bar. The ice cream is squeezed through this opening. A machine pushes a stick into the ice cream. Then a hot wire slices through it. The wire cuts off exactly enough ice cream to make one bar. The slice of ice cream drops onto a stainless steel plate, which is carried away by a moving belt called a **conveyor.** Meanwhile, the next bar is being formed.

As bars of vanilla ice cream drop from the extrusion head, a conveyor carries them to the next part of the factory.

Every step in this process is timed perfectly. The ice cream bars come out of the machine like clockwork, one after the other. Each of the factory's production lines makes thousands of bars an hour, twenty hours a day. That's a lot of ice cream treats!

One production line can make many kinds of ice cream novelties. It can make round bars or bars shaped like animals. It can even make ice cream bars with sections in different flavors. All the workers have to do is change the extrusion heads and use a different recipe for the mix.

An ice cream factory isn't the only place where you might see extrusion in action. Just as soft ice cream can be forced through an extrusion head to create a certain shape, other soft materials can be shaped the same way. Extrusion is used to make metal pipes, rubber and plastic hoses, specially shaped breakfast cereals, and many other objects.

Two kinds of mix and an extrusion head with several openings are used to make these treats.

27

After the ice cream bars have been formed, they travel on the conveyor through a **hardening chamber.** The steel plates move along a spiral track through the freezer. The hardening chamber is extremely cold. Within a few minutes, the ice cream is so hard that if you dropped it on the floor, it would shatter. If you touched it, it would freeze your skin. It's cold enough to stay frozen while it's coated with chocolate, wrapped, and packed into boxes.

A set of metal fingers grips each wooden stick as the treats come out of the hardening chamber.

The machine dips each bar into a tub of warm, melted chocolate coating. Sometimes the liquid coating also contains crunchy bits of cookie or nuts.

As the bars travel along the production line, the coating hardens. The extra chocolate drips off into a gutter.

After the bars are dipped (left), any extra liquid coating drips into a gutter (above).

Finally, another machine seals each treat in a colorful wrapper. The wrappers have already been printed on a long roll of plastic, like a huge roll of paper towels. As the treats pass through the machine, it folds a wrapper around each one.

A hot knife seals both ends of the wrappers and cuts them apart. Each bar is fully wrapped and separate from the others.

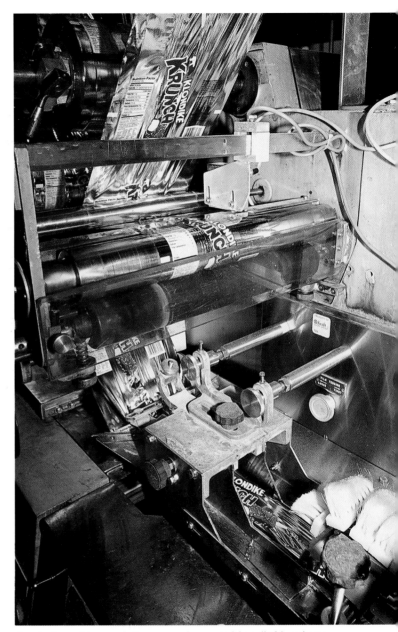

Treats travel toward the wrapping machine (left), where they are covered and sealed tight (above).

Next, each treat passes through a very sensitive metal detector. The factory can't allow any tiny metal pieces from the machinery to get into the ice cream. If there's any metal in an ice cream bar, an alarm sounds. The detector shoves the bar off the line.

Checking the treats with a metal detector is another way to be sure they are safe to eat.

Because they are fragile and oddly shaped, novelties are packed by hand. A group of workers at the end of each production line pack them. Brenda Spruill, Dorothy Rasheed, and their coworkers quickly put the right number of treats into each box.

Even after the treats are wrapped, the workers who handle them still wear gloves and hairnets.

A few of the treats return to a familiar place—the quality assurance lab. Technicians take several finished boxes from each batch. They unwrap the ice cream and melt it. Then they test it to make sure no harmful bacteria have escaped the pasteurization process. Workers can't ship a batch of ice cream out of the factory until the lab technicians say it's okay.

A final check at the quality assurance lab

The boxes of treats travel through a series of machines that automatically close them and seal them with glue and tape. Workers load the boxes into cardboard shipping cartons and place them on another conveyor. Swinging gates called **traffic cops** keep the cartons from running into each other or backing up on the line.

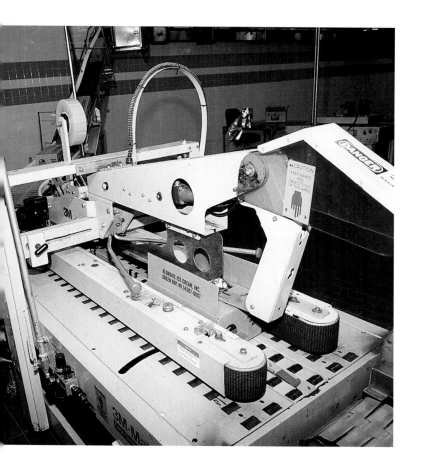

A box of treats is sealed by a machine (left), then packed into a shipping carton and sent down the line (above).

The conveyor carries the cartons to the **cold-storage room.** Inside, it feels like a cold winter morning in Alaska. Harry Davis stacks the cartons onto portable wooden platforms called pallets. To stay warm, he has to wear heavy winter clothing, even in summertime. And the company makes sure he takes a warm-up break every half hour.

The chill of the cold-storage room can make frost form on a worker's hat and mustache.

The whole production process, from the time the soft ice cream comes out of the freezer until the cartons of finished treats reach the cold storage room, takes less than half an hour.

The ice cream doesn't stay in the storage room very long. Once the quality assurance lab says the ice cream treats have passed their tests, the cartons are loaded onto big refrigerated trucks. The drivers take the cartons to a refrigerated warehouse. From there, the ice cream is shipped by truck to stores all over the country.

Refrigerated trucks carry the treats from the factory to a cold-storage warehouse, and then to stores.

The Factory at Night

If you've ever cooked a meal in your kitchen, you know that cleaning up afterward is an important part of the job. Cleanup at an ice cream factory has to be done every day. During the day, all the workers help by wiping up spills. But cleaning the whole factory is the job of the workers on the third shift, or night shift.

The workers on the third shift spend part of their time making ice cream. Then they shut down the machines. They wash and disinfect everything in the factory, inside and out. They scrub the floors, the walls, and the machines. Even the floor drains are cleaned.

Washing the hardening chamber

Fortunately, the workers don't have to take the machines apart to clean them on the inside. The insides of all the machines are cleaned with a system called **clean in place,** or CIP. Very hot water is mixed with detergent and disinfectant. Then it's pumped through the vats, pipes, and other equipment, including the freezers.

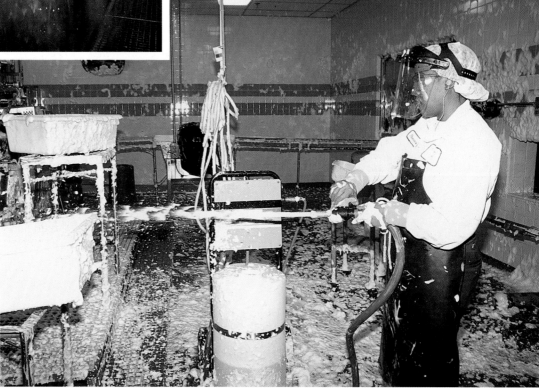

It's a good thing the machines can be cleaned in place (above). Washing other parts of the factory can be messy (right).

Clean and shiny, the stainless steel machines are ready for another batch of mix.

Everything is blasted clean. Then hot rinse water removes any traces of the cleaning chemicals. By the time the workers are finished, the entire factory is sparkling. All the machines are ready to start making ice cream once again.

Unwrap an ice cream bar. It seems like such a simple food. But think about all the hard work that went into making it. Picture the careful workers and complex machines that created this dessert for you. Maybe someday you'll have a chance to make ice cream novelties yourself, test them for quality, or even invent a delicious new recipe. Wouldn't that be a treat?

More about Ice Cream

Books

Busenberg, Bonnie. *Vanilla, Chocolate, and Strawberry: The Story of Your Favorite Flavors.* Minneapolis: Lerner Publications, 1994. This book for older readers describes the plants and processes that bring us the most popular dessert flavors in the world.

Dickson, Paul. *The Great American Ice Cream Book.* New York: Atheneum, 1972. A detailed history of ice cream, this book for older readers also provides recipes and instructions for making ice cream at home.

Fallon, Peggy. *The Best Ice Cream Maker Cookbook Ever.* New York: HarperCollins, 1998. This recipe book shows how you can make rocky road, mocha, and even eggnog ice cream in your own kitchen with an ice cream maker.

Jaspersohn, William. *Ice Cream.* New York: Macmillan Publishing Company, 1988. Black-and-white photographs show the process of making ice cream at a factory in Vermont.

Krensky, Stephen. *Scoop after Scoop: A History of Ice Cream.* New York: Atheneum, 1986. From the ancient Egyptians to modern factories, Krensky describes the history of America's favorite treat.

Neimark, Jill. *Ice Cream!* New York: Hastings House, 1986. Packed with ice cream trivia, this book also includes recipes and describes the modern "ice cream wars."

Websites

Edy's Fun and Games
<http://www.edys.com/fun/index.html>
Edy's company website features games and a personality test based on your favorite ice cream flavor.

The History of Good Humor-Breyers
<http://www.icecreamusa.com/history/index.html>
Good Humor-Breyers Ice Cream invites you to learn about the history of ice cream treats from the Good Humor bar to the popsicle.

The Ice Cream Parlour
<http://www.dsuper.net/~zaz/icecream/frame.html>
This site features recipes for ice cream, yogurt, gelato, and other frozen treats.

University of Guelph Ice Cream
<http://www.foodsci.uoguelph.ca/dairyedu/icecream.html>
This site is packed with details about ice cream history, production methods, recipes, and much more.

Coffee-Can Ice Cream

Here's a recipe for ice cream treats you can make at home.
You will need:

2 cups whipping cream
½ cup sugar
½ teaspoon vanilla
   extract
1 cup miniature
   chocolate chips
large coffee can with plastic
   lid (approx. 2 lbs. 7 oz.)
small coffee can with plastic
   lid (approx. 13 oz.)
½ cup rock salt
3–4 cups crushed ice
plastic wrap
2 rubber bands
8 small plastic cups (about 5 oz.)
8 wooden ice cream sticks
crushed cookies or chopped nuts
   (optional)

1. Mix the cream, sugar, and vanilla in a bowl. Wash the small coffee can and lid with soap and water. Pour the cream mixture into the can. Add the chocolate chips.

2. Put the lid on the small can. Cover the top of the small can with plastic wrap. Use a rubber band to secure the wrap.

3. Put a shallow layer of crushed ice on the bottom of the large can. Sprinkle a very thin layer of rock salt on top. Put the small can into the large can.

44

4. Layer crushed ice and rock salt around the small can. Each layer of ice should be about an inch thick, with a very thin layer of rock salt on top. The layers should reach all the way to the top of the large can.

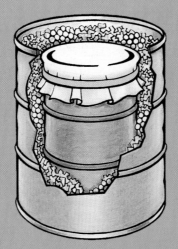

5. Put the lid on the large can. Cover the top of the large can with plastic wrap. Use a rubber band to secure the wrap.

6. Sit on the floor with a friend. Roll the large can back and forth for 15 minutes.

7. Open the large can carefully. Remove the small can. Wipe off the outside of the small can before opening it.

8. Spoon the ice cream into the plastic cups. Fill each cup about halfway. Put a wooden ice cream stick in the center of each cup so that the end sticks out far enough to hold in your hand.

9. Put the cups in the freezer. Freeze for at least 8 hours. For best results, freeze overnight. The ice cream will be frozen but still slightly soft.

10. To eat a treat, sprinkle a few drops of warm water on the outside of the cup to loosen the ice cream. Holding the stick, gently slide the treat out of the cup. For an even tastier dessert, roll the treat in cookie crumbs, nuts, or more chocolate chips. Enjoy!

Makes 6–8 treats.

Glossary

agitator: a metal paddle in the center of a vat in a factory. An agitator spins back and forth to stir the contents of the vat.

bacteria: tiny living things that can cause food to spoil or make people sick

batch processing: a common factory method in which a batch of material is mixed, prepared, and turned into a final product by a series of machines. While one batch is being processed by the machines, workers prepare the next.

butterfat: the fat that milk or cream contains

clean in place: a way to clean machinery without having to take it apart and wash the pieces separately

cold-storage room: a refrigerated warehouse or storage building

condensed milk: milk that has been heated until more than half the water has turned to steam and been removed

conveyor: a system of belts and rollers that carries things from one part of a factory to another

dasher: a spinning blade in the center of an ice cream maker

emulsifier: a substance that helps butterfat coat the tiny air bubbles in ice cream. Emulsifiers make ice cream creamier and easier to shape.

extrusion head: the part of a factory machine that shapes the final product by squeezing it through an opening

flavor vat: a large container where flavorings such as vanilla or chocolate are added to ice cream mix

hardening chamber: the part of an ice cream factory where ice cream bars are frozen to an extremely cold temperature

loading bay: a garage-like section of a factory where trucks are loaded or unloaded

mixing station: a large vat where basic ice cream mix ingredients, such as milk, cream, and sugar, are combined

novelties: the dairy industry's name for individual ice cream treats, such as ice cream on a stick

overrun: air that is added to liquid ice cream mix as it freezes to make the ice cream soft, smooth, and scoopable

pasteurize: to heat milk or other foods in order to kill bacteria that cause spoiling or disease

production floor: the part of a factory where a product is made

production line: a series of machines that make a product in a factory

quality assurance lab: the part of a factory that tests a product to make sure it is safe and meets other standards

raw milk: milk that comes directly from farm animals and has not yet been pasteurized

stabilizer: a substance that prevents large ice crystals from forming in ice cream while it is stored

traffic cops: swinging gates that keep items on a conveyor from running into each other or getting backed up

If you have an ice cream maker at home, you can try this fruity concoction. You will need:

2 cups grape juice
2 cups half and half
$\frac{1}{2}$ cup sugar
juice of 1 lemon

Mix the ingredients in a bowl until the sugar is completely dissolved. Taste the mixture. If it isn't sweet enough, stir in another teaspoon of sugar. Follow your ice cream maker's directions to freeze.

Index

Acknowledgments

Additional photographs courtesy of: © Bettmann/Corbis, pp. 11, 13; U.S. Patent #5,601, p. 12; © Good Humor-Breyers Ice Cream, p. 14 (left); © The Mahoning Valley Historical Society, Youngstown, Ohio, p. 14 (right). Illustrations on pp. 9, 44–45 by Laura Westlund, © 2001 by Carolrhoda Books, Inc.

The author and photographer would like to thank the Good Humor-Breyers Ice Cream Company for helping with this project and generously allowing us to photograph their ice cream factory in Richmond, Virginia. Thanks to Ben Benjamin, Dave Deeslie, Peter Mendelson, and Janet Burke for reviewing our manuscript, and to Tamra Strenz and Jennifer Stout, who helped us get the permissions we needed.

Special thanks to Mike Casstevens, plant manager; Vic Miller, Harvey Thompson, and Bob Josephson, production supervisors; and all the other employees who patiently maintained their good humor while we asked questions and took photographs, and who kindly agreed to appear in this book. Thanks to Shannon Zemlicka, Michael Tacheny, and everyone at Lerner Publishing Group. Finally, thanks to Karen Merricks and Schoolfield Elementary School for arranging for the photographs of kids enjoying ice cream.